KT-599-974

Behind the Scenes
GYMNASTICS

Christopher Hilton

CHERRYTREE BOOKS

A Cherrytree Book

Photography Allsport UK Ltd

Designed by Les Dominey
Produced by
Autumn Publishing Ltd
Appledram Barns
Chichester, West Sussex

Line drawings by Carter Beatty,
West Sussex

First published 1991
by Cherrytree Press Ltd
a subsidiary of
The Chivers Company Ltd
Windsor Bridge Road
Bath, Avon BA2 3AX

6836
1

Copyright © Cherrytree Press Ltd 1991

British Library Cataloguing in Publication Data
Hilton, Christopher
  Gymnastics.
  1. Gymnastics
  I. Title II. Series
  796.44

  ISBN 0-7451-5110-8

Printed in Singapore by Imago Publishing Ltd

CONTENTS

Starting out

Children can start gymnastics at virtually any age, but most coaches feel that for girls the best age is between six and seven years, and for boys between six and nine years.

Talent scouts in some Eastern European countries pick out boys and girls of five years old as possible gymnasts. The scouts' selection depends on the child's body type, family history and whether or not he or she has passed a set of physical tests. After a trial period of eight months where the children train for 12 hours a week, a long-term programme is planned and the number of hours is increased. By the time they are six years old, children are training for as many as 20 hours a week.

In Britain and America at that age, six to eight hours a week is considered enough to lay the foundations for good gymnastics. By the age of nine or 10 years, the time spent training increases to at least 12 hours a week. A promising 12-year-old will train for 18 to 20 hours.

Gymnastics requires fitness, practice and sometimes a helping hand. Here we see Nadia Comaneci of Romania (in green leotard) training with friends as they learn to balance on the beam.

Olga Korbut (USSR), the little gymnast who attracted the world's attention to the sport in 1972 at the Olympic Games in Munich.

Dedication

Because so many hours are spent training in the gym, gymnastics demands total commitment. This is especially true for boys, who have to practise on, and master, six pieces of apparatus. The girls have only four, which is still very demanding.

From the very first lesson, the most important qualities that aspiring gymnasts need are perseverance and dedication. To be a gymnast, youngsters must be prepared to be separated from their friends – unless their friends are also gymnasts!

If a gymnast is going to progress, he or she must train for three or four hours a day. This may mean arriving at the gym at 6 am every day and, unless they live within walking distance, someone, (probably Mum or Dad!) will have to transport them and, two hours later, pick them up and take them to school.

After school, a gymnast will often return to the gym for another training session. Later, when other children have had supper and done their homework, the tired gymnast will just be arriving home. While most children are settling down to watch television or getting ready to go out with friends, a gymnast must eat, and do his or her homework. There is not much time left to do anything else before going to bed.

The young gymnast who decides to make gymnastics a career has to work hard at an early age, and give up most other interests.

Scholarships

In America, each year the National Boys Invitational is held in Pennsylvania. At this competition, coaches offer scholarships for colleges and universities to the most talented competitors. There is no similar competition for girls; they tend to emerge through sports or gymnastics clubs. There are also special summer camps for boys and girls where the best coaching is available.

In Toronto, Canada, there is a special school for gymnasts where the government helps to support competitors financially. This is particularly important because it enables gymnasts to travel the often vast distances within their own country, as well as abroad.

Age Group squads

In Europe, there is no selection system in schools because they do not hold gymnastics competitions. Sometimes a scheme is set up to encourage children to work for gymnastics badges or awards, but youngsters who are thinking of taking gymnastics seriously, have to join a gymnastics club and go to a gymnasium in their own time and at their own expense.

At gymnastics clubs in Britain, for example, promising gymnasts are put in regional Age Group squads for under 12s, under 15s and under 18s. They take part in Age Group competitions and if they continue to be successful they join a senior national squad and spend many of their weekends training at sports centres around the country.

Karine Colomb (FRA) shows she has learnt grace and balance as she competes in the French Young Hopefuls Championship at Grenoble in 1989.

Coaches and managers

Promising youngsters, who decide to make a career of gymnastics, will need constant advice from a coach.

Coaches

Gymnastics coaches at international levels are among the most highly trained sporting specialists in the world. At local levels, coaches tend to be interested parents or teachers, who have taken up coaching.

When a coach watches beginners, he or she looks for good co-ordination, variety of movement, strength and mental application. The right build and upright posture are important, too. An experienced coach can see immediately if a child has potential as a gymnast.

Ideally, a coach has only two or three pupils. Standards at competition level are so high that training has to be quite intense. A coach is not, however, able to watch each pupil all the time and so it is usual for gymnasts to make their own notes detailing their movements and performance. These notes, which can be referred to away from the class, help coaches and gymnasts to be aware of the pupils' weak points as well as progress.

Gymnasts make notes on every movement and performance they work on. These notes are helpful to coach and pupil when preparing for a competition.

The coach's role

To establish a suitable routine, the coach and gymnast work on a long-term plan and update the routine at the end of every year. When it comes to perfecting a new element in a routine, the gymnast must work with the coach for hours on end, day after day, on a movement which, when it is finally included in the routine, may last no longer than four or five seconds.

The role which a coach plays in the life of a young gymnast is more than that of an instructor. Coaches are there to give advice, comfort and encouragement. They plan the gymnasts' careers, adjust schedules according to how their skill is progressing and judge the right time to enter competitions. They keep a constant note of each gymnast's height, weight and physical development.

It is a coach's job to make sure that pupils have 'aerobic' fitness. The coach gradually increases the gymnasts' work-load with more and more repetitions. This ensures that the heart, respiratory and circulatory systems are strong so that a nine-year-old, for instance, can complete a 70-second floor exercise and still have plenty of breath left.

Team coach

When gymnasts reach competition standard and represent their country, they will work with the team coach who will help and advise them at competitions. For example, the team coach will decide how much time should be spent on the warm up, and be at hand to help the men gymnasts onto the rings.

The coach often finds the best way of describing an action is to demonstrate it. This coach's pupil still has some finishing touches to improve upon before the competition.

Team manager

Teams are led by a team manager. The team manager is responsible for checking that competitors and all other members of the team (coaches, reserves and possibly a doctor or physiotherapist) have passports and visas when travelling to competitions abroad. The team manager makes the travel arrangements and hotel bookings. Some gymnasts may have special diets and the manager must ensure that the hotel caters for these. A meeting will be held before a competition to advise the team on travel and hotel arrangements.

Diet

Gymnasts must keep their weight down. Those who get too heavy will reach a point where they cannot cope with their own body weight. Exercises that involve jumping or hanging become more difficult the heavier a gymnast gets. The greatest danger among girl gymnasts is not overweight, but underweight caused by a dangerous condition called anorexia nervosa. This is

The manager of a team has a lot to organize before a competition. One of his jobs is to kit out the gymnasts with a team uniform. The Romanian team are seen here wearing their country's national colours.

Bela Karolyi, the Romanian who first discovered Nadia Comaneci, moved to America where he teaches aspiring gymnasts. Of the young hopefuls lined up here only a few will make the grade.

where eating less and less results in a person not wanting to eat any food at all. This may happen when a gymnast (or anyone else) tries to shed weight without seeking proper professional advice.

A gymnast needs plenty of fibre, which is found in fruit, vegetables and wholemeal bread. Food high in proteins, such as eggs, milk, fish and meat are important for building muscle tissue. When a body is worked hard it needs energy, which gymnasts get from carbohydrates found in pasta, bread and cereals. For a burst of energy before a particularly strenuous event a glucose sweet or a small amount of chocolate may be eaten. As competitions last all day, it is sometimes difficult for a competitor to know when to eat a meal, but a light breakfast and lunch is usually advised.

At the gym

The warm up

The warm up is extremely important as the body performs better when muscles and joints are loosened, and the possibility of injuries caused by trying to stretch tight, cold muscles is reduced.

At competitions or in class, gymnasts start with warm up exercises such as skipping, running, jumping and arm-circling which involve the whole body. Many coaches recommend repeating the same exercises several times. This gets the blood flowing through the body.

Some classes then continue with conditioning and go on to weight-lifting and push-ups. These preliminary exercises are important, but they should not be too hard or the gymnasts will tire quickly.

Apparatus

The whole idea of gymnastics is that the body makes certain shapes as perfectly as possible. These shapes appear again and again on different pieces of equipment.

Germany's Benno Gross on the pommel horse at the 1984 Los Angeles Olympics. Trousers and vest allow a gymnast free movement while the magnesium sulphate on the hands prevents them from slipping.

For men

The floor: is 12 square metres of carpet laid on a slightly sprung base.

The vault: is a padded horse 1.35 metres high and 1.6 metres long, without handles.

The parallel bars: consist of two bars made of wood supported by a metal frame. Both the bars are the same height from the floor at 1.7 metres. Gymnasts can request how far apart they want the bars to be.

The pommel horse: looks like the vault, but it has two raised handles in the middle.

The rings: are two wooden circles hung on steel cables and are 2.5 metres above the ground.

The high bar: often called the horizontal bar, is a minimum of 2.4 metres long, stands 2.5 metres high, and is made of steel.

Terry Bartlett (GBR) on the vault at the 1988 Olympic Games at Seoul.

For women

The floor: is the same as for men.

The vault: is 1.2 metres high and is the same length as for the men. It is, however, turned sideways.

The beam: is 5 metres long, but at the top it is only 10 centimetres wide. It stands on supports 1.2 metres above the ground and is covered with material, usually suede.

The asymmetric bars: sometimes called the uneven parallel bars. These are two fibreglass rails, one 1.5 metres above the ground and the other 2.3 metres. Like the men's parallel bars the distance between the bars can be adjusted to suit individual gymnasts.

Additional apparatus

Mats are used in a gym at each piece of apparatus. There are thick, non-slip mats for vaulting onto, deep, soft crash mats under high bars, and thinner, regulation mats around the beam in case of a fall. Crash mats are essential when a gymnast is learning moves or gaining confidence while practising difficult ones.

The springboard is made of wood. It can be adjusted to suit the length of a run-up and the chosen position of the gymnast for take-off. This piece of apparatus is used for mounting the high bars, the beam (optional) and for vaulting.

A powerful run-up and a good take-off from the springboard are essential for a successful vault.

Men's exercises

The programme on the floor must last between 50 and 70 seconds and involve tumbles, somersaults and linking movements. A good rhythm is important and the gymnast should show how supple he is. He should also cover as much of the floor area as he can.

The vault exercise is divided into seven movements – the run-up, the hurdle-step on the springboard, the jump itself, the flight onto the vault, the push from the vault, which takes the gymnast to a second flight into the air and, finally, the landing. In flight, the gymnast turns or somersaults. On landing, the feet must be together and the body held still. The gymnast is allowed only one chance at the vault.

On the parallel bars the gymnast swings and launches himself into flight. He must hold balances for two seconds.

The pommel horse, often regarded as the most difficult exercise of all, is a programme of non-stop swinging. This involves making subtle, demanding movements without the legs touching the horse. Strength comes from the arm muscles and the grip of the hands on the two handles while the legs describe circles.

The rings also need strength from the arms and hands, and the gymnast swings his body up and over. He performs handstands and one outright test of strength, the crucifix, where his arms are stretched out to either side in line with his shoulders. This position must be held for two seconds.

The high bar exercise is a dramatic whirling of motion with swings moving to and fro without any stops. The gymnast should change his grip and let go of the bar completely at least once during a routine, swing over it and catch hold of the bar again.

Bulgarian, Stoian Delchev, demonstrates the need for strength on the rings. It is not easy to get into a position like this and it must be held for two seconds.

Women's exercises

The floor exercise is essentially the same as for men, but with one significant difference: the programme is accompanied by music and allows gymnasts to show a sense of rhythm and artistic flair. Some girl gymnasts attend ballet classes as part of their training and use dance steps in the floor and beam exercises.

The vault exercise is the same as for the men, but women are allowed two attempts with the higher score counting. In the finals of this event, however, they must perform two different vaults and this time the average of both marks is the score.

The beam is a difficult exercise, because the apparatus is so narrow. However, many complicated moves are performed on it during a 70 to 90 second programme. Balance is the key – if a gymnast does a back somersault she has only 10 centimetres to land on. (During the 1983 World Championships all the finalists, except the medal winners, fell off!) In this exercise, gymnasts must link their movements, which include leaps, pivots, hops and rolls, and avoid repetition. Planned pauses are allowed before a difficult movement, but they must not be too long.

The asymmetric bars is a programme of about 30 seconds and both bars must be used. The gymnast

Protective equipment

It is essential for gymnasts to take care of their hands, particularly in exercises involving the bars. They use hand lotion to keep the palms soft and, for exercises that involve grasping the apparatus, they wear handguards made of suede. These guards help to prevent blisters and hard skin forming. Many gymnasts also strap up their wrists under the guard straps.

Gymnasts dip their hands into a white chalky powder, called magnesium carbonate. This powder reduces the chance of sweaty hands slipping around or off the bars.

During training practice on the asymmetric bars, the girls wear foam or rubber padding across the lower part of the stomach to guard against bruising. For safety reasons, women gymnasts always tie their hair back and remove any jewellery when working in the gym or competing. Both men and women keep their nails short and make sure that they look neat and tidy — particularly in front of the judges.

Kathy Johnson (USA) on the beam, where she won a bronze medal at the 1984 Los Angeles Olympics.

should make about 12 to 14 different moves, including changes of grip and direction, hanging, swinging and somersaulting. The exercise must be flowing and any pauses are penalized.

Clothing

Correct clothing which fits properly is essential, as loose clothing can catch on apparatus and cause an accident. As individuals, gymnasts buy their own and the choice of colour and style is up to them. At national level, clothing is supplied to the team and the design will often include the national emblem.

When taking part in team competitions, men and women wear costumes in the same colours. Points may be deducted if regulations on dress are not followed.

The correct clothing for men is a vest, long white trousers which fasten under the instep with an elastic strap, socks and special aerobic shoes, or socks only. For exercises on the floor and vault, men can wear shorts.

Women must wear a leotard with long sleeves. They usually wear aerobic shoes without socks, and some perform in bare feet. Aerobic shoes are made of thin leather with small supple rubber pads on the heels and soles for grip. For warm up exercises, men and women wear tracksuits.

Wu Jiani of China competing on the beam. She has wrapped tape round her ankles to support them.

The championships

As the popularity of gymnastics has grown over the years so has the number of important championships. Many nations have their own invitation international tournaments, such as the America Cup in New York, the Chunichi Cup in Tokyo and the Champions All tournament in Birmingham, England. There are also the larger, multi-sport games such as the Pan-American Games and the Mediterranean Games which include gymnastics as part of their programme. All these may be competed in before a gymnast reaches the European and World Championships, and Olympic Games. It is a big circuit and the better a gymnast gets, the more competitions he or she can expect to be in.

A gymnastics arena laid out for the start of a competition.

The European Championships are held in different venues in Europe with cities bidding to host them. Any European country is eligible to compete. The World Championships are staged every alternate year by the sport's governing body, FIG, which stands for Fédération Internationale Gymnastique (in English this means the International Gymnastics Federation). The Olympic Games take place every four years. The selection of nations to compete in the Olympics is based on the results of the previous year's World Championships. The top 12 men's and women's teams compete and the 13th to 15th placed countries can send three gymnasts, the 16th to 18th can enter two.

Taking part in the Olympic Games is the highlight of any gymnast's career and it is a long struggle from club and regional competition to get there.

Apart from team competition, there is the World Cup, an annual event, which was started at Wembley in 1975 for top gymnasts to compete as individuals.

Organizing a competition

Preparation for any major competition starts well in advance because it takes a lot of time to plan and co-ordinate an event which must run smoothly. At the World Championships, for example, there are about 200 officials involved and they must all know exactly what their duties are and when to perform them.

The hall and facilities

The hall is generally an all-purpose sports hall, big enough to accommodate all the gymnastic equipment. If the area around the apparatus were cramped it would make life difficult for the gymnasts. It would also spoil the artistic and dramatic effect by distracting the eye of the spectator.

The hall may seat up to 10,000 spectators and have room for television cameras and equipment, as well as technicians. Special commentary cubicles have to be provided for commentators from all around the world. A press room is also essential. From here journalists can send their stories by telephone, telex and fax. Some championship venues have a 'dark room' where

Under the spotlights, Susan Cheeseborough's (GBR) movements on the asymmetric bars are closely watched by a large crowd. This competition was held at Wembley Arena in London.

photographers can process their films; and there is often a special service which is used for sending photographs by wire to newspaper offices round the world, so that pictures can appear in papers the next day.

J796·44 21

An interview room is available so that journalists can speak to the gymnasts after they have performed. As the official language is English some teams bring interpreters with them. But, often the more experienced competitors know enough English to cope with interviews and press conferences themselves.

Sponsorship

Without the help of commercial sponsorship, many competitions would not take place. Various organizations, from sports manufacturers to newspapers, provide money to help cover the costs of staging events. In return, their names are prominently displayed round the hall and are associated with a flourishing sport that has family spectator appeal. In this way the sport is assisted financially and the companies benefit from worldwide advertising.

Judges

Many judges are parents who have become involved in the sport through the participation of their children. Others are ex-coaches or past competitors. They start judging at club level and work their way up through county, regional and national levels to international competitions. Exams are taken at each stage and to qualify as an international gymnastics judge, they have to pass exams in both theory and practice. There are no professional judges, in that they are not paid for their work. They do receive expenses for food, travel and accommodation however.

In women's events there are four judges at each piece of apparatus (six in international competitions). They are supervised by a head judge and an assistant, known as a Scientific Technical Collaborator. These two officials are needed to stop judges giving marks that are too far apart. Judging the artistic content of a performance is so much a matter of personal opinion that judges have to agree on a comparable scale.

In the men's events at national level and below, there are four judges and a master judge for each piece of apparatus. At international competitions there are again four judges and these are supervised by a superior judge and an assistant judge.

Judging and scoring

Judging begins as soon as a gymnast comes forward to start an exercise and ends the instant the gymnast is stationary at the finish. Judges want to see the degree of difficulty each gymnast attempts and how supple and strong he or she is, how well the moves are made during an exercise and the way the movements are linked together. They watch to see what mistakes are made and whether the exercise breaks down at any point. They also judge how original a programme is.

If a coach is not satisfied that the judging has been fair he or she may challenge the mark and query it with a jury of appeal. At international competitions, however, this is no longer allowed.

The judges have watched Ecaterina Szabo of Romania perform on the vault and now they have to make their decision.

Judging at major competitions

At major competitions – the European, World and Olympic championships – events are divided into three sections, the team competition, the combined event for individuals and the apparatus finals.

Team competition

The team competition is very important because it forms the basis for later stages of the championship, as well as being a competition in its own right. Gymnasts do compulsory exercises on the first day and voluntary exercises on the second. The six highest marks of each team are added together to give a team total. All the gymnasts in the winning team receive gold medals and the same applies for the team that receives silver medals for coming second, and bronze for third place.

Combined event

This event determines which male and female gymnasts are the best all-rounders. Only 36 gymnasts are allowed to take part in this event. No more than three per country can qualify from the team competition. Ranked according to their scores in the team competition, gymnasts do their voluntary exercises again.

Apparatus finals

On each piece of apparatus a competition is held between the eight gymnasts who scored the highest marks on that particular piece of apparatus in the team competition. However, each country can put only two gymnasts forward per piece of apparatus.

Scoring

Exercises are either compulsory, which means that the gymnast has to do specific movements in a set pattern; or they are voluntary, where the gymnast can create his or her own routines within specific guidelines.

Voluntary exercises

Judges look at several areas during a gymnast's exercises with an International Code of Points to guide them. The Code tells judges how many points either to deduct or add as bonuses. Judges can award a maximum of 10 points.

As a guide, a breakdown of points for scoring for men is given on the next page:

Difficulty	3.40 points
Combination	1.60 points +
Execution	4.40 points
	9.40 points
ROV	0.60 points +
	10.00 points

There are four grades of *difficulty*:

A basic	0.20 points
B reasonably difficult	0.40 points
C difficult	0.60 points
D very difficult	0.80 points

Left: Mary-Lou Retton (USA) won the individual gold medal at the Los Angeles Olympics in 1984.

Right: The scoreboard shows a score that is extremely difficult to achieve – the perfect 10.00 – won by Mary-Lou Retton on the floor exercise at Los Angeles.

At national level, a programme must contain a mixture of A B and C grades. The inclusion of a D-graded move is a bonus.

Combination means the skill in linking all the moves to create one exercise. Points for *execution* are given for accuracy and style. The bonus points come under the heading ROV which stands for risk, originality and virtuosity, each of which is worth 0.20 points

The *risk* involved is not a question of danger. It is the complication of a move, like a change of grip. If a

competitor does not carry the move through he risks losing points.

Originality can be in creating a new move or new interpretation of combining various elements.

Virtuosity means the flair in executing moves, to make a performance stand out as superior to the other competitors.

Women are marked in a similar way, with the judges looking for various grades of difficulty, originality, variety and style. One point is given for the general impression the gymnast has made in her performance.

A perfect 10.00 can be achieved if the bonus points, such as those for ROV, are given. Some points are deducted automatically – for falling off a piece of apparatus (0.50), stepping out of the floor area (0.30), sitting down on landing after a dismount (0.50), including an extra swing on the bars to gain impetus (0.30 points).

When a gymnast's score is calculated, the highest and lowest marks presented by the judges are eliminated. The remaining marks are added together and divided by two or four (depending on the total number of judges) to find the average. This is done to prevent a judge showing national bias by marking 'his or her' gymnast too high, or maybe a rival from another country too low.

The difference between the remaining middle scores must not be too great, either. If the judges are giving marks that are too far apart, the head judge asks them to check their scoring in case someone has missed a fault or judged too harshly. Again, this is to make sure that judging is fair and accurate.

Compulsory exercises

For set exercises the judges start with a mark of 9.40 for men and 9.60 for women, and deduct points for faults or lack of skill. Each gymnast must do exactly the same movements in a set pattern so there is no question of originality. It is possible to get a perfect score of 10.00 points, however, as fractions of a mark can be added as a bonus for a particularly difficult move which was well executed.

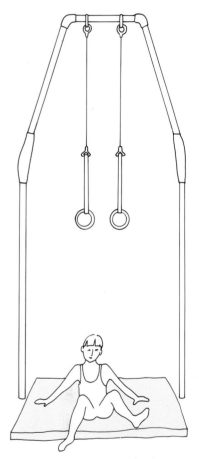

If a gymnast sits down on landing after a dismount, the judges will automatically deduct 0.50 points from his or her score.

Making it to the top

The route to the top is much the same for any gymnast. Each region has its own competitions and, if a gymnast does well, he or she will go on to take part in further competitions until they reach national standard. At national competitions the best gymnasts are picked out to represent their country abroad in a squad, or team. There are international junior squads of 12 to 14-year-olds and senior squads for those over 14 years of age.

Oksana Omeliantchik of the Soviet Union chalks up in preparation for her next event. It can be a lonely and daunting moment as the gymnasts concentrate on what lies ahead.

The big moment

What is it like to compete in a big contest, such as the World Championships? The great championships are always full of tension and, because there are many competitors with a lot going on all at the same time, they can be confusing too.

The competitors are divided into groups and are given a timetable so that they know exactly when they are competing on each day. As a rule, the less successful countries will go first, the better ones later to provide an exciting finale.

At the stadium, the gymnasts get changed and go to the warm up area. The team coach decides how much warming up they should do and helps to calm the competitors' nerves.

Just before the time comes for a gymnast to be led out by the coach, he or she may eat a bar of chocolate to give them extra energy. The gymnast is called to compete and it is time to enter the arena.

Waiting to begin an exercise is often worse than actually competing. The area where the gymnasts perform may be raised so that it looks like a stage and round the edge of it press photographers crouch and close-up television cameras loom. The competitor steps up on to the stage and smears his or her hands with the chalky magnesium carbonate. Well known gymnasts will receive applause when their name is announced, but they will not acknowledge it as they are trying to compose themselves mentally for what lies ahead. When a competitor is ready to start, he or she will raise an arm. If it is the women's floor exercise the music begins almost immediately.

This is the big moment and suddenly the gymnast is deep into the routine, concentrating so hard, moving so quickly that he or she hardly hears the applause that comes after a particularly difficult move.

When the exercise is over, the gymnast walks down the shallow steps from the stage and is met by one of the team's coaches. One of the gymnasts drapes a tracksuit top round the competitor's shoulders while the others gather round to watch for the scoreboard's results.

As the championships unfold and the teams do their

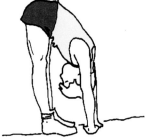

Warming up exercises include stretching and touching the toes which help to loosen tight, cold muscles and avoid injury. These exercises are essential, especially when a gymnast is preparing to compete.

Daniele Silivas of Romania is all smiles as she celebrates her team's victory at the 1988 Seoul Olympic Games.

different exercises, the tension rises. Every gymnast knows how well he or she is doing, where they stand in the marking and what they will have to do in the next exercise to bring their marks up and beat their rivals. Everyone is trying to improve, to gain places.

These are emotional moments and the joy of winning a medal cannot be beaten. In the excitement of the ceremony, the competitors will not ask for any other reward than to have done their best and made it to one of the top positions.

The rewards

There are big rewards in gymnastics if you reach the top. There is the satisfaction of having been the best – or among the best – and this will last for the rest of a gymnast's life.

Fame and success can attract money-making opportunities. Mary-Lou Retton (USA) made a million dollars using her name to advertise well known companies, such as McDonalds. Kurt Thomas from Indiana State University, who won six medals at the World Championships in 1979 (making him the most successful American male gymnast), became a television commentator.

Soviet gymnasts are rewarded by being able to travel

The American men's team after they won the 1984 Los Angeles Olympic team competition. Since this victory, three members of the team are reported to be millionaires, and two, Mitch Gaylord and Bart Connor, were offered parts in films.

abroad, something their fellow citizens are rarely allowed to do. Nadia Comaneci has had a film made about her life and Olga Korbut was given a Volga car as well as an apartment with two rooms of her own – both items of great luxury. Korbut said: 'Thanks to gymnastics I became famous, met many people and visited lots of places. It helped me to cope with the training. Seeing people hard at work by a furnace, at mines or on the railways inspired me to new heights. It helped to turn me into a celebrity.'

However hard the competition is, gymnasts learn a great deal about themselves and their bodies. That alone makes it worthwhile. If a gymnast respects the sport, the result will simply be pleasure – enormous pleasure.

Olga Korbut, the gymnast who attracted the world's attention to the sport is grateful for the rewards gained from being a top gymnast.

Index